DK WORKBOOKS

1st Grade

Problem Solving

Author Linda Ruggieri

Educational Consultant Melissa Maya

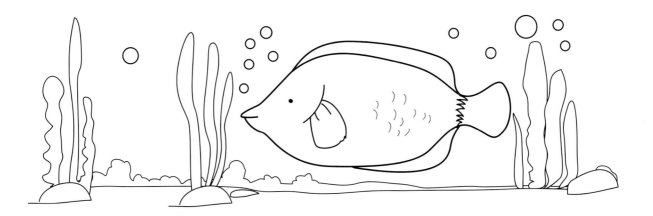

Penguin Random House

Senior Editor Cécile Landau
Editor Nishtha Kapil
US Editors Allison Singer, Lindsay Walter
Project Art Editor Dheeraj Arora
Senior Art Editor Ann Cannings
Art Director Martin Wilson
Producer, Pre-Production Dragana Puvacic
Producer Priscilla Reby
DTP Designer Dheeraj Singh
Managing Editor Soma B. Chowdhury
Managing Art Editor Ahlawat Gunjan

First American Edition, 2016
Published in the United States by DK Publishing
345 Hudson Street, New York, New York 10014

Copyright © 2016 Dorling Kindersley Limited
DK, a Division of Penguin Random House LLC
16 17 18 19 20 10 9 8 7 6 5 4 3 2 1
001–285372–Feb/2016

A catalog record for this book
is available from the Library of Congress.
ISBN: 978-1-4654-4479-0

DK books are available at special discounts when purchased
in bulk for sales promotions, premiums, fund-raising, or
educational use. For details, contact: DK Publishing Special
Markets, 345 Hudson Street, New York, New York 10014
SpecialSales@dk.com

Printed and bound in China.

All images © Dorling Kindersley Limited
For further information see: www.dkimages.com

A WORLD OF IDEAS:
SEE ALL THERE IS TO KNOW

www.dk.com

Contents

This chart lists all the topics in the book. Once you have completed each page, stick a star in the correct box below.

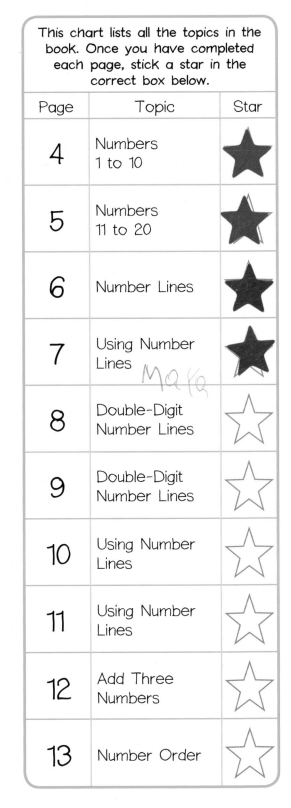

Learn the number words for 1 to 10.

Draw a line to match the number word on each balloon with the correct number from the list in the middle.

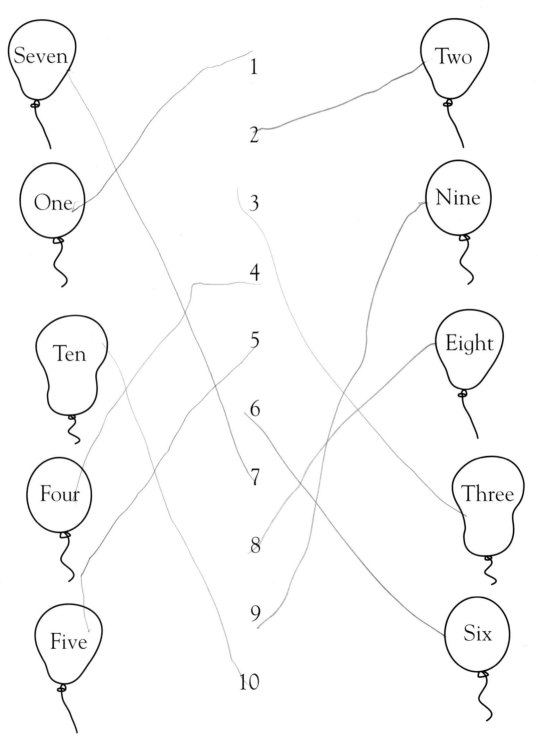

GOAL

Learn the number words for 11 to 20.

Help Bruno the dog reach his doghouse. Find the bones that have the number words from 11 to 20 on them. Color them in to show Bruno the way.

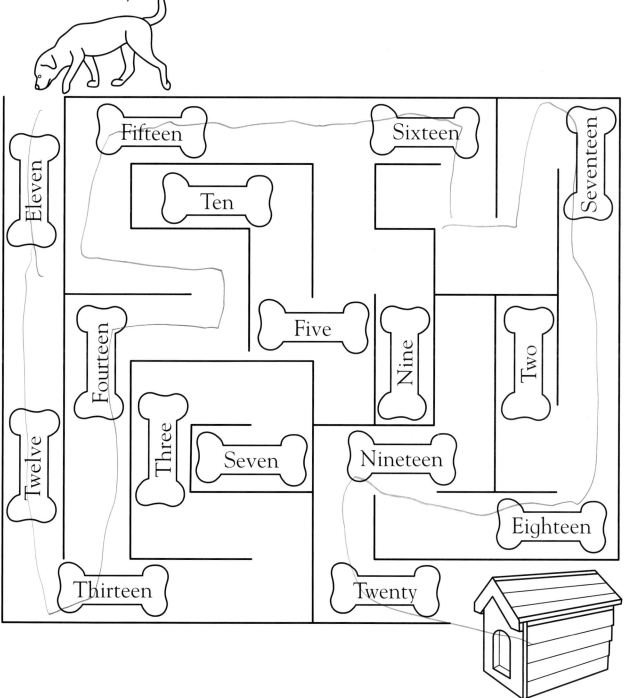

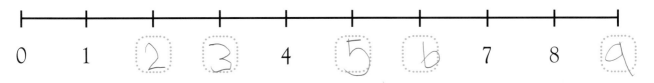

GOAL

Learn to count along a number line.

Fill in the missing numbers on the number line below.

0   1   2   3   4   5   6   7   8   9

Now circle the correct number to answer these questions.

If you start at 3 and count forward two numbers, which number do you land on?

5   7   8

If you start at 0 and count forward three numbers, which number do you land on?

2   3   4

If you start at 5 and count forward four numbers, which number do you land on?

7   8   9

Find two even numbers on the line and write them here.

Find two odd numbers on the line and write them here.

Learn to solve addition problems using a number line.

Jake, Sara, and Don visit the farmers' market with their dad. Count along the number line below to find the answer for each problem.

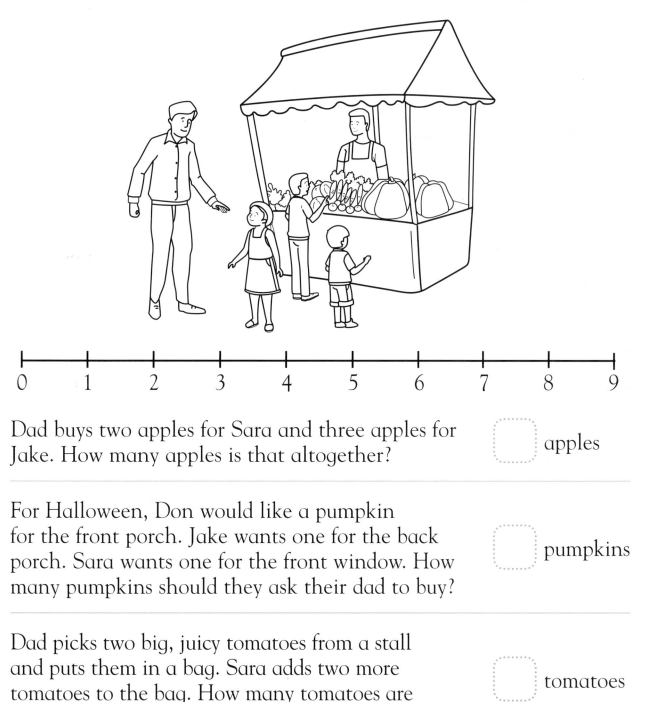

Dad buys two apples for Sara and three apples for Jake. How many apples is that altogether?

☐ apples

For Halloween, Don would like a pumpkin for the front porch. Jake wants one for the back porch. Sara wants one for the front window. How many pumpkins should they ask their dad to buy?

☐ pumpkins

Dad picks two big, juicy tomatoes from a stall and puts them in a bag. Sara adds two more tomatoes to the bag. How many tomatoes are in the bag altogether?

☐ tomatoes

⭐ Double-Digit Number Lines

GOAL

Learn to use a number line with two-digit numbers.

Write the missing numbers on this number line.

10 11 12 13 14 15 16 17 18 19 20

Now solve these problems, using the number line.
Write your answers in the boxes.

If Bunny starts at 10 and hops forward two
numbers, which number will he land on?

If Bunny hops to 14 and then he makes two more
hops forward, which number will he land on?

If Bunny rests on 17 and then makes one more hop
forward, which number will he land on?

At 18, Bunny smells some juicy carrots. How many more
hops must he make to reach the carrots at number 20?

8

$×÷%=$+?—×÷%=$?+—%×÷=$+?—×÷%

Double-Digit Number Lines ★

GOAL

Practice counting two-digit numbers along a number line.

Use the number line to find the answers to the clues below.

10 11 12 13 14 15 16 17 18 19 20

I am 18 plus two more.

I am two more than 13.

I am one more than 17.

I am three more than 13.

I am ten more than ten.

I am three more than 16.

I am two more than 15.

I am one more than 13.

$ × ÷ % = $ + ? — × ÷ % = $? + — % × ÷ = $ + ? — × ÷ %

9

Learn to solve subtraction problems using a number line.

Chloe the cat has nine kittens. Help her keep track of them by filling in the missing number in each rhyme. Use the number line to figure out the answers.

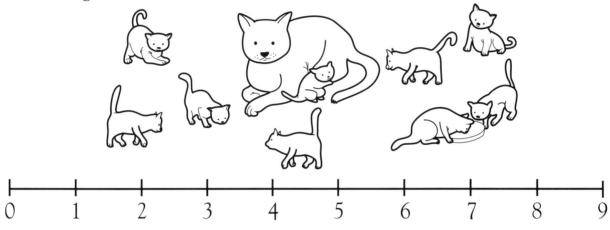

```
├──┼──┼──┼──┼──┼──┼──┼──┼──┤
0  1  2  3  4  5  6  7  8  9
```

Three kittens are playing, but one runs away.

Now just ☐ of the kittens are left to play.

Five kittens are drinking from a pan.

But ☐ take off to see a tall man.

Two of the kittens stay by the pan.

Seven kittens climb up a tree.

☐ climb down.

And now the tree has three.

Nine kittens run outside chasing a mouse.

☐ kittens are left in the house.

Practice subtraction with a double-digit number line.

The Rams basketball team has won six games in a row. The scores are given below. Count backward on the number line to figure out the difference in points scored in each game.

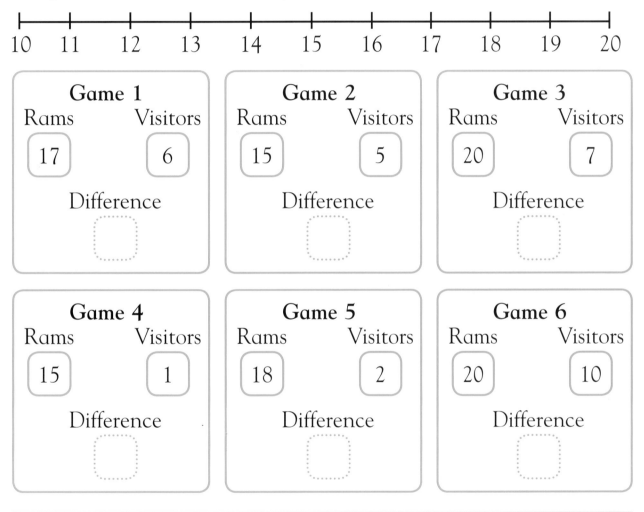

	Rams	Visitors	Difference
Game 1	17	6	
Game 2	15	5	
Game 3	20	7	
Game 4	15	1	
Game 5	18	2	
Game 6	20	10	

Now answer these questions.

Which game shows a difference of 14 points? ....

Which game has a difference of 11 points? ....

Which game did the Rams win by the most points? ....

★ Add Three Numbers

Learn to solve problems that involve adding three numbers.

Flash the fish is swimming through the salty sea.

Write out the number sentence to solve each of these problems.

Four whales swim up to Flash. Then four rays arrive, followed by two clown fish. How many sea animals are with Flash now?

4 + 4 + 2 = 10 sea animals

Flash swims past three sea anemones. He then sees five more sea anemones. Later, he spots another four. How many sea anemones does Flash see in all?

☐ + ☐ + ☐ = ☐ sea anemones

Flash sees 15 starfish on the ocean floor. Then he spots two jellyfish and a small blue fish next to them. How many sea animals does Flash see on the ocean floor?

☐ + ☐ + ☐ = ☐ sea animals

Learn about number order when adding.

Write the answers to each pair of equations. **Note:** The numbers being added are the same in each pair.

$7 + 2 + 1 =$ 10 $2 + 7 + 1 =$ 10

$6 + 1 + 0 =$ 7 $0 + 6 + 1 =$ 7

$5 + 3 + 1 =$ 9 $3 + 1 + 5 =$ 9

What do the answers tell you about the order of numbers (or addends) in an addition problem?

....

Carrie and Mack go to a carnival.

Carrie takes two rides on the Ferris wheel, one ride on the Space Blaster, and three rides on the Tilt-a-Whirl.

Mack takes three rides on the Ferris wheel. Then he rides the Tilt-a-Whirl twice and the Space Blaster once. Who takes the most rides? **Hint:** First write the number sentences to arrive at the answer.

Carrie's rides   Mack's rides

....

....

Practice solving addition problems.

In each set of problems, circle the number sentences that match the words.

Set 1

Christian buys five pencils, three markers, and six notebooks. How many items does he buy altogether?

5 + 8 + 6 = 19   5 + 3 + 6 = 14

Allie buys five headbands, six hairbrushes, and three combs. How many items does she buy altogether?

3 + 6 + 3 = 12   5 + 6 + 3 = 14

Set 2

Mr. Jones buys four pizzas, five salads, and six drinks. How many items does he buy altogether?

4 + 5 + 6 = 15   4 + 5 + 4 = 13

Mary's mom orders six pieces of chicken, four kinds of biscuits, and five drinks in a restaurant. How many items does she order?

6 + 5 + 6 = 17   6 + 4 + 5 = 15

What do you notice about the number sentences you circled for each set of problems?

....

....

GOAL

Learn to simplify three-number addition problems by first adding the numbers that equal ten.

Solve these equations.

Hint: First circle two numbers that add up to ten and combine them. The first one has been done for you.

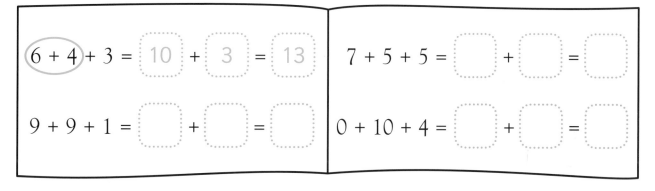

$$(6 + 4) + 3 = \boxed{10} + \boxed{3} = \boxed{13} \qquad 7 + 5 + 5 = \boxed{} + \boxed{} = \boxed{}$$

$$9 + 9 + 1 = \boxed{} + \boxed{} = \boxed{} \qquad 0 + 10 + 4 = \boxed{} + \boxed{} = \boxed{}$$

Write number sentences to solve these problems.

Remember: First circle and combine two numbers in your number sentence that add up to ten.

Bob saw six rattlesnakes at the zoo. He also saw four coral snakes and three garden snakes. How many snakes did Bob see altogether?

$$\boxed{ + +} = \boxed{} + \boxed{} = \boxed{} \text{ snakes}$$

Carmen read five books about horses. Jane also read five different books about horses, followed by two books about ponies. How many books did the girls read altogether?

$$\boxed{ + +} = \boxed{} + \boxed{} = \boxed{} \text{ books}$$

Learn to count by tens.

Four crows are gathering twigs to build their nests. Solve these problems. Show your work in the box. The first one has been done for you.

Each crow gathers a bundle of ten twigs. How many twigs do they collect altogether?

40

twigs

4 bundles of 10 = 10 + 10 + 10 + 10 = 40

One crow uses her bundle of twigs to build a nest. How many unused twigs do the crows now have altogether?

twigs

Another crow decides to make a larger nest. She uses twice as many twigs as the first crow did. How many twigs does she use?

twigs

The four crows go out to gather more twigs. This time they collect two bundles of ten sticks each. How many twigs is that altogether?

twigs

GOAL

Learn to solve problems using equations with unknown, or "mystery," numbers.

Solve these problems. Show your work in the box.
The first one has been done for you.

A spider caught ten flies in its web. After eating a few, it had four flies left. How many flies did the spider eat?

6

flies

4 + ? = 10

10 − 4 = 6

Some ants are on the ground.
Seven more ants are on a bush.
If there are 12 ants altogether,
how many ants are on the ground?

ants

Thirteen bees are flying around a garden.
A few minutes later, there are 16 bees
flying around. How many more bees
have entered the garden?

bees

Jamie sees 11 ladybugs. They are in two
groups. The first group has five ladybugs.
How many ladybugs are there in the
second group?

ladybugs

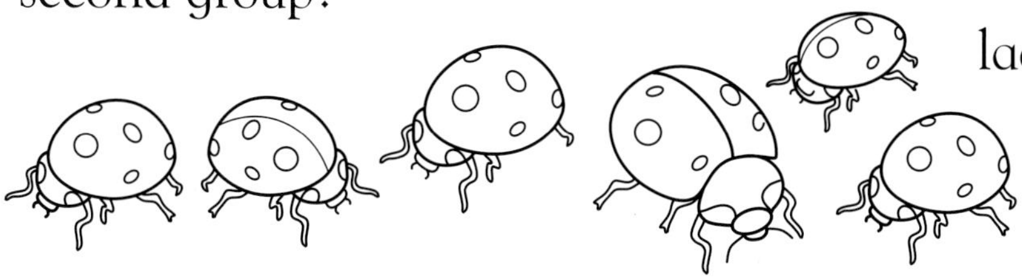

GOAL

Learn to count and write numbers up to 120.

Karl has a bucket of berries for his pet parrot. Help him reach his pet by filling in the missing numbers on the stones along his path.

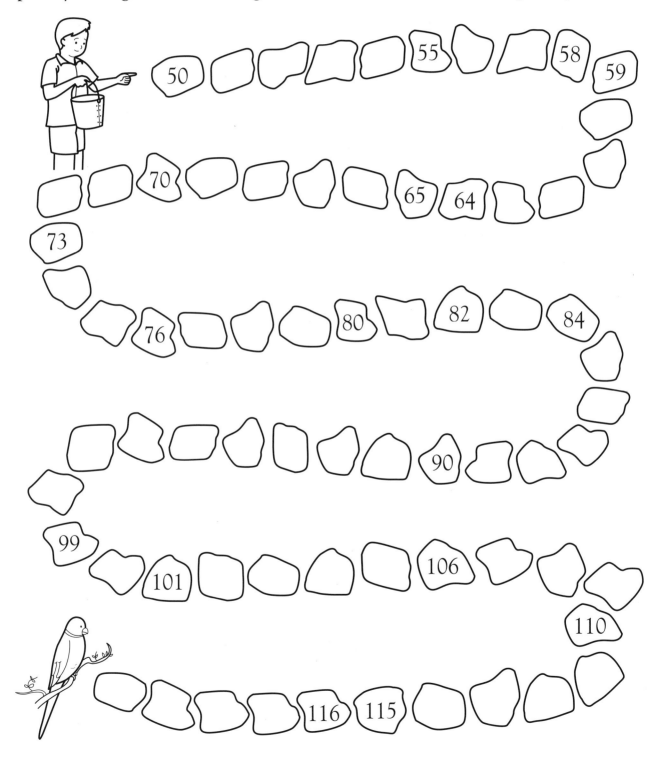

$ × ÷ % = $ + ? — × ÷ % = $? + — % × ÷ = $ + ? — × ÷ %

Practice matching two-digit numbers with their number words.

How many buttons are in these two jars altogether? Circle the correct answer.

Seventy-five

Eighty-five

70 buttons   15 buttons

Write ninety-nine as a number.

Circle the number word that is made up of five tens and eight ones.

Fifty-eight   Eighty-five

Circle the correct number word for 62.

Seventy-three   Sixty-two

Which page in this book is the picture of a horse on? Circle the correct answer.

Eighty-one

Sixty-one

80   81

More or Less

GOAL

Learn to use the symbols for greater than (>) and less than (<) to compare numbers.

Look at the numbers on each pair of fish below. Then write the correct symbol to compare the numbers.

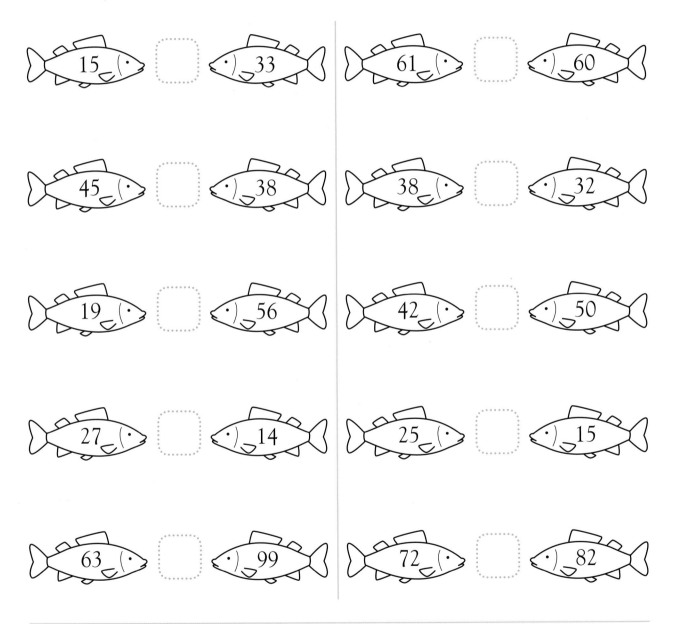

15 ☐ 33	61 ☐ 60
45 ☐ 38	38 ☐ 32
19 ☐ 56	42 ☐ 50
27 ☐ 14	25 ☐ 15
63 ☐ 99	72 ☐ 82

Look at the fish again. If a fish has a number that is greater than 30, color it in.

Two-Digit Numbers

Learn three ways to represent two-digit numbers.

Fill in the empty boxes on the chart.

Word	Numeral	Blocks
Thirty-two		
....	25	
Sixteen	16	
....		

GOAL

Learn about the place values of tens and ones in two-digit numbers. For example, the numeral 23 is made up of 2 tens and 3 ones.

Tens	Ones	
2	3	= 23

These children are learning about place values. On the table are small blocks to represent ones and longer blocks to represent tens.

Todd uses the blocks on the table to make a model for the number 27. He lays out two long blocks to show 2 tens. How many small blocks must he add to show the ones?

☐ small blocks

The teacher shows the children a drawing of some dots to illustrate the number 87. Her drawing shows seven dots for the ones. How many rows of ten dots does it show?

☐ rows

Charlene writes the number 45 on a piece of paper. She then draws some dots to illustrate the number. She draws a group of five dots for the ones. What else must she draw to illustrate the number 45?

Do the numbers 14 and 41 have the same number of tens and ones?

GOAL

Learn about place value in two-digit numbers.

These pirates are digging for treasure. Treasure boxes, buried deep in the sand, contain gold. Each box has a code on it showing how much treasure is inside it. Use the key to work out how many bars of gold are in each box.

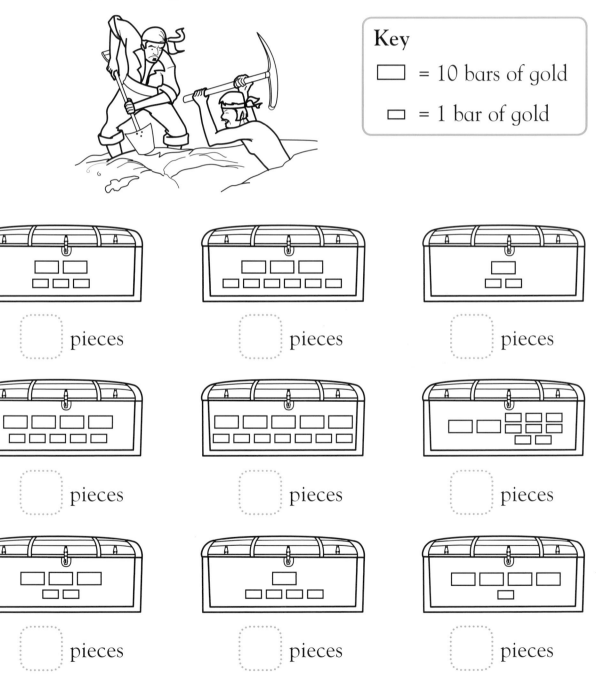

Key

☐ = 10 bars of gold

☐ = 1 bar of gold

pieces pieces pieces

pieces pieces pieces

pieces pieces pieces

Learn to identify ten more or ten less than a two-digit number.

Draw a line to match each spaceship to the star with the correct answer.

45

64

25

51

100

Ten More or Ten Less ★

Practice solving problems by calculating ten more or ten less than a two-digit number.

Solve these problems. Try to use mental math to figure out the answers, if you can.

Juan counts 22 birds in the branches of a tree. He then sees another ten birds flying by. How many birds does Juan see altogether?

birds

Jane counts 18 fence posts as she rides her bicycle down the street. As she rides back, she counts ten more fence posts on the other side of the street. How many fence posts does Jane count altogether?

fence posts

Mike counts 13 yellow flowers in his garden and ten yellow flowers in his neighbor's garden. How many yellow flowers does he count altogether?

yellow flowers

Shep spots 16 butterflies near a path. Ten of them fly away. How many butterflies are left?

butterflies

Jason sees 12 squirrels near a tree. As Jason approaches, ten of them run away. How many squirrels are left?

squirrels

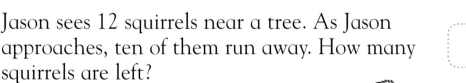

★ Add Two-Digit Numbers

GOAL

Practice addition with two-digit numbers.
Hint: First add the ones together, then add the tens.

$$
\begin{array}{r}
2|2 \\
+\ 1|4 \\
\hline
6
\end{array}
\rightarrow
\begin{array}{r}
2|2 \\
+\ 1|4 \\
\hline
3\ 6
\end{array}
$$

Write the answers.

$$
\begin{array}{r}
42 \\
+\ 20 \\
\hline
\end{array}
\qquad
\begin{array}{r}
31 \\
+\ 51 \\
\hline
\end{array}
\qquad
\begin{array}{r}
45 \\
+\ 32 \\
\hline
\end{array}
\qquad
\begin{array}{r}
12 \\
+\ 33 \\
\hline
\end{array}
\qquad
\begin{array}{r}
10 \\
+\ 15 \\
\hline
\end{array}
$$

Now solve these problems. Show your work in the box.

Pete stacks 70 cans of peas on the shelves of his store. He also stacks 24 cans of corn. How many cans does Pete stack altogether?

☐ cans

Pete moves and restacks 50 cans of tomatoes to make room for another 30 cans, which he adds to the shelf. How many cans does he move and stack in all?

☐ cans

$\$\times\div\% = \$ + ? - \times \div \% = \$? + - \% \times \div = \$ + ? - \times \div \%$

Practice solving addition problems with two-digit numbers.

Tim, Teresa, and their mom visit the garden center. Solve these problems. Show the equations you use to figure out your answers. The first one has been done for you.

Tim buys 12 pink roses and 15 yellow roses. How many roses does he buy altogether?

27

roses

$$12 = 10 + 2$$
$$+15 = 10 + 5$$
$$20 + 7 = 27$$

Teresa buys 25 daisies and four tulips to go with them. How many flowers does she buy altogether?

flowers

For a party, Mom needs 42 small plants for the tables and 17 flower displays. How many items does she need altogether?

items

Mom orders 22 bushes for the backyard and 25 bushes for the front yard. How many bushes does she order altogether?

bushes

Subtract Two-Digit Numbers

Practice subtraction with two-digit numbers.
Hint: First subtract the ones, then subtract the tens.

$$\begin{array}{r} 3\,|\,6 \\ -\,1\,|\,4 \\ \hline 2 \end{array} \rightarrow \begin{array}{r} 3\,|\,6 \\ -\,1\,|\,4 \\ \hline 2\ 2 \end{array}$$

Help rake the leaves by solving the problem on each leaf.

$$\begin{array}{r} 55 \\ -\,34 \\ \hline \end{array}$$

$$\begin{array}{r} 39 \\ -\,25 \\ \hline \end{array}$$

$$\begin{array}{r} 56 \\ -\,24 \\ \hline \end{array}$$

$$\begin{array}{r} 68 \\ -\,18 \\ \hline \end{array}$$

$$\begin{array}{r} 57 \\ -\,46 \\ \hline \end{array}$$

$\$ \times \div \% = \$ + ? - \times \div \% = \$? + - \% \times \div = \$ + ? - \times \div \%$

Subtract Two-Digit Numbers ★

Practice solving subtraction problems with two-digit numbers.

Some friends collect baseball game tickets, baseball cards, and baseballs. Solve these problems. Show your work in the box. The first one has been done for you.

Matt collects 70 baseball cards. Jack collects 50. How many more cards than Jack does Matt collect?

20

cards

$$70 = 70 + 0$$
$$-50 = 50 + 0$$
$$20 + 0 = 20$$

In a year, Joan collects 92 game tickets and Mary collects 50. How many more tickets than Mary does Joan collect?

tickets

Luis collects 22 baseballs. Mike collects 12. How many more baseballs than Mike does Luis collect?

baseballs

Nancy has 18 baseballs. Her dad gave her ten, and her brother gave her the rest. How many baseballs did Nancy's brother give her?

baseballs

GOAL

Learn the names and values of coins.

For each row, circle the coin on the right that has the same value as the total number of coins on the left.

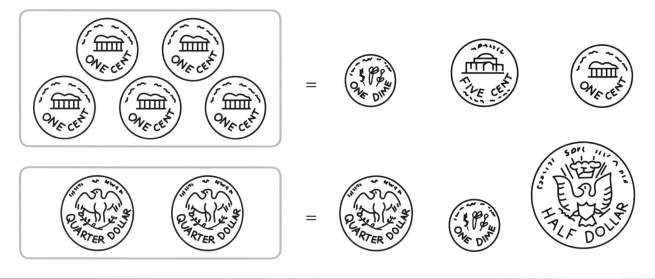

Tom and Mary empty out the contents of their piggy bank. Here are the coins they have.

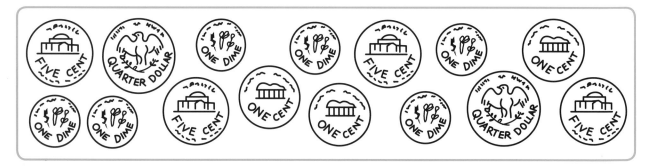

How many of each type of coin do Tom and Mary have?

pennies   nickels   dimes   quarters

Learn to solve money problems.

Cole has five pennies. How much money does he have?

Look at these coins. Circle the dime.

Circle the total value of these coins.

5¢   13¢   6¢

Look at the piggy bank. How much money is in there?

Kim has one dime and two pennies. Which of these items can she buy? Circle it.

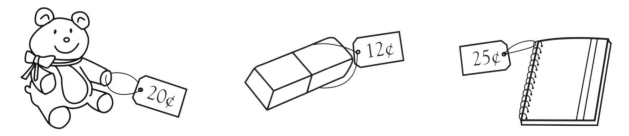

20¢   12¢   25¢

Learn to measure length using a common object, such as a penny.

Baseball bats are lying on the floor.

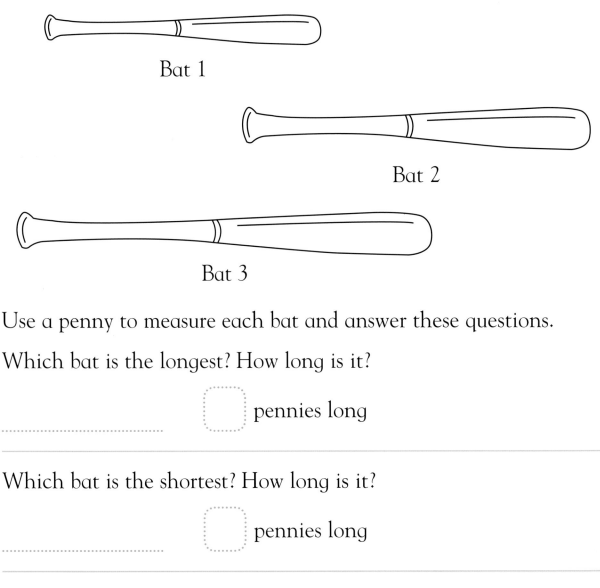

Bat 1

Bat 2

Bat 3

Use a penny to measure each bat and answer these questions.

Which bat is the longest? How long is it?

.... ⌂ pennies long

Which bat is the shortest? How long is it?

.... ⌂ pennies long

Which bat is 6 pennies long?

....

Learn to measure length in inches.

Use a ruler marked in inches to find the length of these objects.

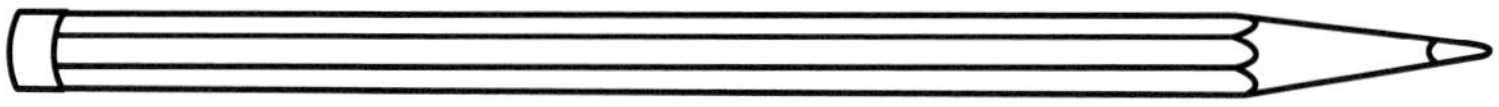

[ ] inches

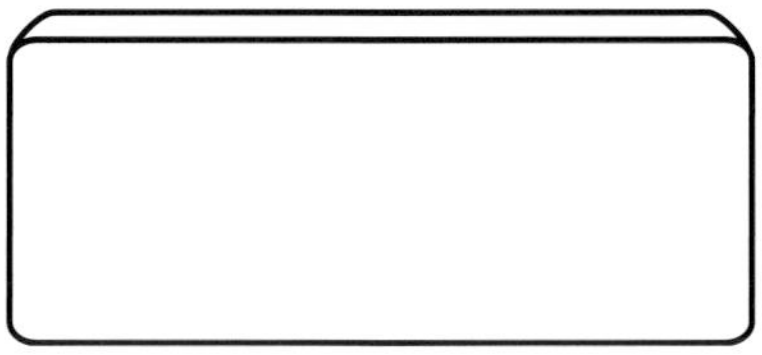

[ ] inches

[ ] inches

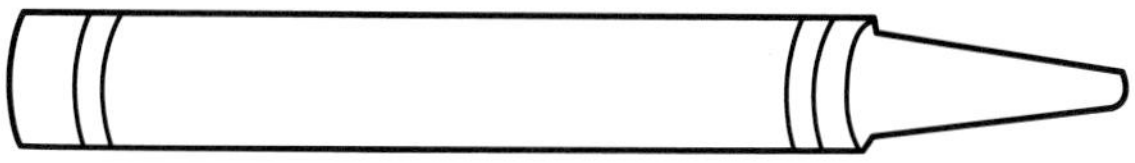

[ ] inches

Now answer these questions.

Which object is the longest? ....

Which object is the shortest? ....

Which object is 4 inches long? ....

GOAL

Learn to measure length in centimeters.

Ruby loves ribbons. Use a ruler marked in centimeters
to help her measure these ribbons for her hair.

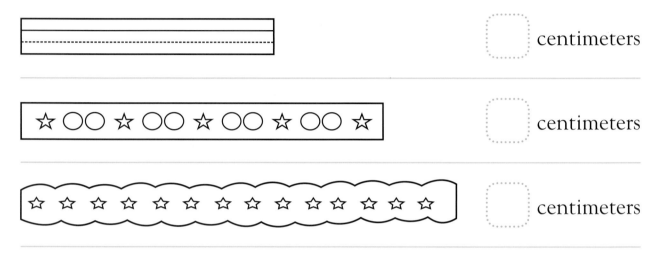

[ ] centimeters

[ ] centimeters

[ ] centimeters

Look at these ribbons and then answer the questions.

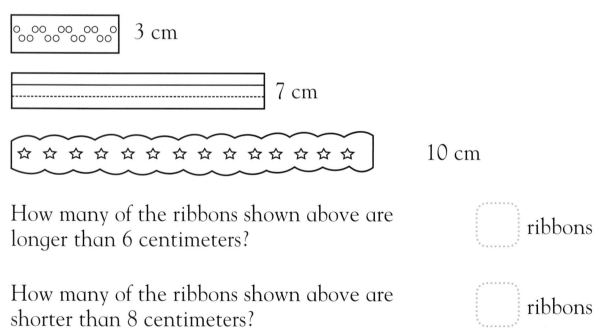

3 cm

7 cm

10 cm

How many of the ribbons shown above are
longer than 6 centimeters?

[ ] ribbons

How many of the ribbons shown above are
shorter than 8 centimeters?

[ ] ribbons

Ruby needs a piece of ribbon that is 10 centimeters long.
Which of the ribbons shown above can she use? Circle it.

Learn about different measurement tools and their uses.

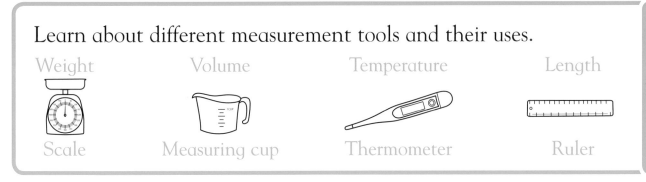

Weight	Volume	Temperature	Length
Scale	Measuring cup	Thermometer	Ruler

Circle the correct picture to answer each question.

Jan wants to weigh some apples. Which one of these tools should she use?

Mom needs one cup of milk to make pancakes. Which of these tools should she use?

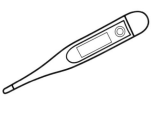

A teacher wants to measure the height of one of her students. Which one of these should she use?

Kim has the flu. Her mom wants to check Kim's temperature. Which one of these tools should Kim's mom use?

Learn to tell the time to the hour and the half hour.

Two o'clock   Three thirty

Show the correct time to match the statements given below. First draw the hands on the analog clock. Then write the time on the digital clock.

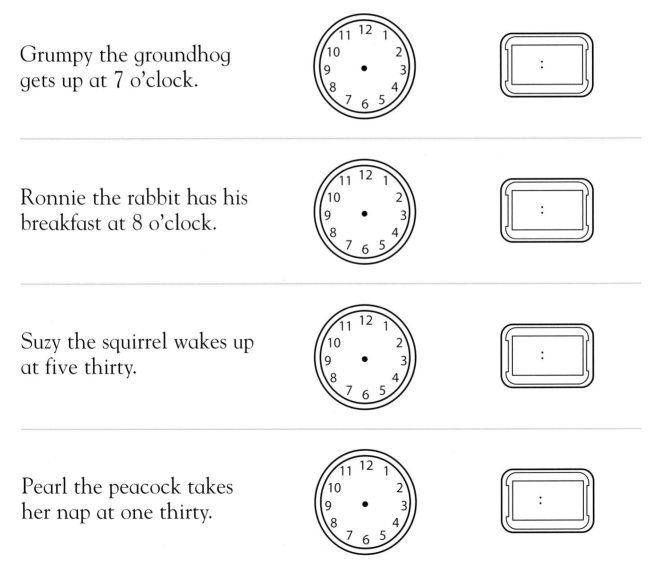

Grumpy the groundhog gets up at 7 o'clock.

Ronnie the rabbit has his breakfast at 8 o'clock.

Suzy the squirrel wakes up at five thirty.

Pearl the peacock takes her nap at one thirty.

Practice telling the time. **Note:** When you say "half past one," it is the same as saying "one thirty."

Match the times written in the box below to the correct clock image. Write the correct time underneath each clock.

11:30	Seven thirty	8:30	2 o'clock	4:00
Nine thirty	10 o'clock		Two thirty	Twelve thirty

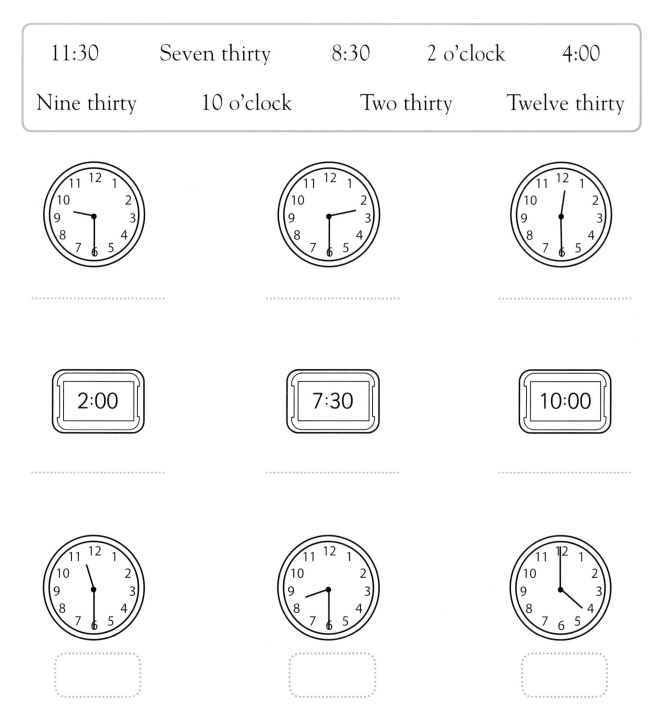

★ Using a Calendar

Learn to read a calendar.

Look at the calendar page below. Then answer the questions that follow.

July

Sunday	Monday	Tuesday	Wednesday	Thursday	Friday	Saturday
		1	2	3	Independence Day 4	5
6	7	8	9	10	11	12
13	14	15	16	17	18	19
20	21	22	23	24	25	26
27	28	29	30	31		

How many Sundays are in the month shown?

Tom's birthday is on July 12. Jo's birthday is on July 16. How many days later than Tom's birthday is Jo's? _____ days

Which day of the week is July 1? ....

Which day comes between Wednesday and Friday? ....

It is July 22. In three days, Mrs. Lee's class is going on a picnic. What day is the picnic on? What will the date be? ....

Practice using a calendar.

Use this calendar page to answer the questions below.

September

Sunday	Monday	Tuesday	Wednesday	Thursday	Friday	Saturday
				1	2	3
4	5	6	7	8	9	10
11	12	13	14	15	16	17
18	19	20	21	22	23	24
25	26	27	28	29	30	

How many days are in September?   days

How many Fridays are in this month?

September 8 is Mary's fourth day back
at school after summer vacation. On
which day and date did school start?

Mark has soccer practice in two days.
Today is September 6. On what day and
date does Mark have soccer practice?

Learn to identify some common 2-D shapes.

Square   Triangle   Oval   Circle   Rectangle

Fill in the missing word in each speech bubble.

I see a shape with four corners and four straight sides. The sides are not all the same length, but opposite sides are. It is a _____.

I see a shape with four corners and four sides that are the same length. It is a _____.

I see a shape that has three sides and three corners. It is a _____.

I see a shape that looks like an egg. It has no corners. It is an _____.

I see a round shape. It has no corners. It is a _____.

$\$ \times \div \% = \$ + ? - \times \div \% = \$? + - \% \times \div = \$ + ? - \times \div \%$

Learn to identify 2-D shapes in the world around you.

Look at these pictures on the wall of an art gallery. They are displayed in a variety of frames. How many frames of each shape can you see? Add this information to the chart below.

Shape	⬜	△	⬭	◯	▭
Number					

Now answer these questions.

Which shape is there the most of? ....

Which three shapes have two frames each?

....

Four of the frames are this shape.
Which shape is it? ....

3-D Shapes

GOAL

Learn to identify some common 3-D shapes.

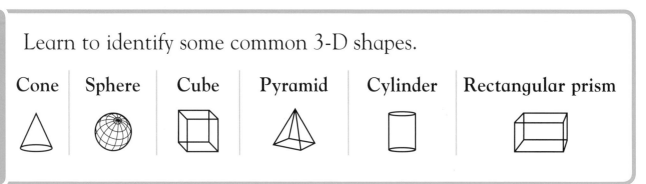

Cone	Sphere	Cube	Pyramid	Cylinder	Rectangular prism

Some of the 3-D shapes in this maze have the wrong labels. Find your way through the maze by following only the 3-D shapes with the correct labels.

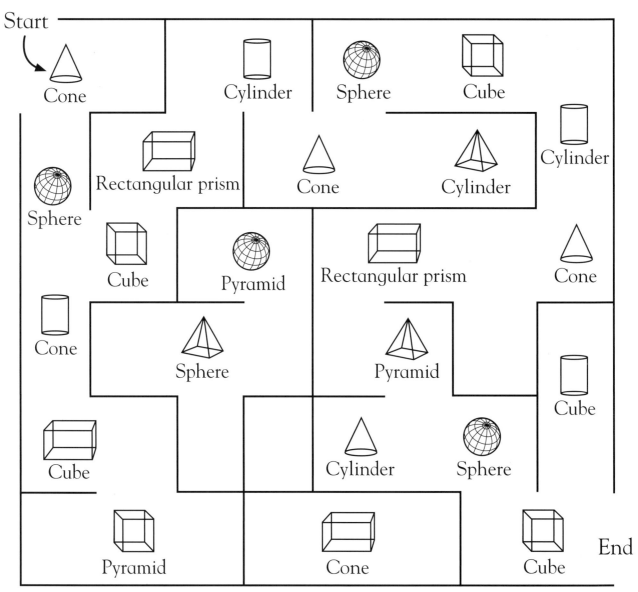

Learn to identify 3-D shapes in the world around you.

Fill in the correct missing word at the end of each of these stories. **Hint:** Look at the 3-D shapes on page 42 to help you.

Jan takes a walk with her sister Liz. They see a baseball in a yard. Jan says, "That baseball is shaped like a ...."

Dad is making lunch for Sara. He opens a can of soup. Sara says that the can has the shape of a ....

Todd's little brother is playing with his alphabet blocks. The faces on the blocks are square. Todd knows that the blocks have the shape of ....

Jim and his mother go to the grocery store. He sees some of his favorite juice boxes on the shelves. They are shaped like ....

Sam goes to a birthday party. He wears a tall party hat with a round opening at the bottom and a pointed top. His friend Chi says, "Your hat has the shape of a ...."

GOAL Learn to use a picture graph to find information.

A class of first grade children were offered fruit after lunch. They had a choice of a banana, an apple, a pear, or an orange. The picture graph below shows how many children ate each type of fruit.

Fruit Children Ate

☺ = 1 child

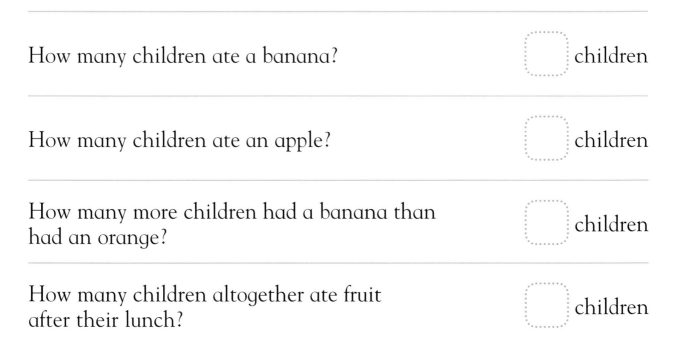

Type of Fruit	Number of Children
Banana	☺ ☺ ☺ ☺ ☺
Apple	☺ ☺ ☺ ☺
Pear	☺ ☺ ☺
Orange	☺ ☺ ☺

Use the information on the picture graph to answer these questions.

Which type of fruit did most of the children choose? ....

How many children ate a banana? ☐ children

How many children ate an apple? ☐ children

How many more children had a banana than had an orange? ☐ children

How many children altogether ate fruit after their lunch? ☐ children

Learn how to show information on a picture graph.

In a school survey, a class of first graders voted for their favorite pizza. Four children voted for cheese pizza. One child chose mushroom pizza. Three chose pepperoni pizza and two chose sausage pizza. Complete the picture graph below to show how many children voted for each type of pizza. Give your graph a title.

....

☺ = 1 child

Type of Pizza	Number of Children

Use your picture graph to help you answer these questions.

Which type of pizza was the least popular? ....

Which type of pizza did most children choose? ....

How many types of pizza does the graph show?

How many more children chose cheese pizza than chose mushroom pizza?   children

GOAL

Learn to find information by looking at a bar graph.

A teacher asked her students to tell her their favorite toy. She then made a bar graph to show the results.

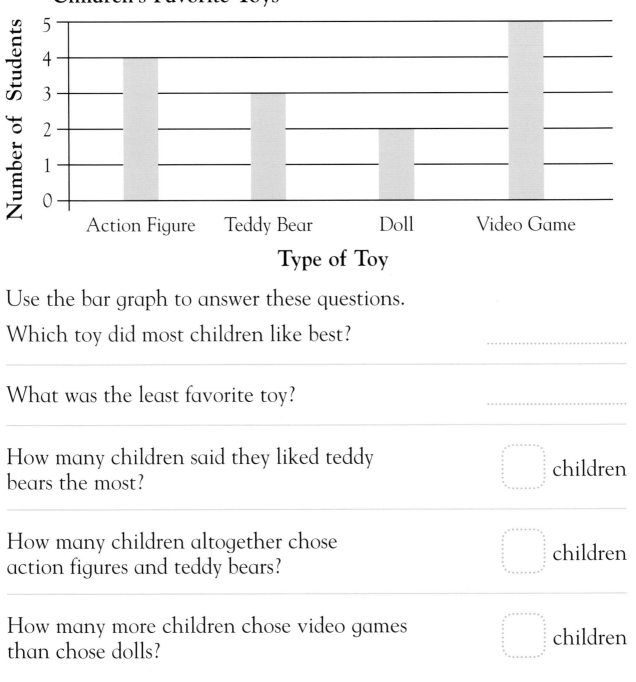

Children's Favorite Toys

Use the bar graph to answer these questions.

Which toy did most children like best? ....

What was the least favorite toy? ....

How many children said they liked teddy bears the most? ☐ children

How many children altogether chose action figures and teddy bears? ☐ children

How many more children chose video games than chose dolls? ☐ children

Learn how to show information on a bar graph.

A group of children had fun blowing bubbles. They blew five large bubbles, six medium-sized bubbles, and seven small bubbles. Complete the bar graph below to show this information. Give the graph a title.

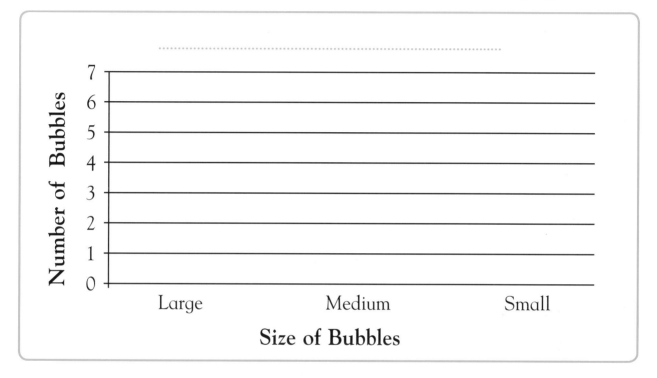

Use the graph to answer these questions.

How many bubbles did the children blow altogether? ⬚ bubbles

How many more small bubbles were there than large bubbles? ⬚ bubbles

How many medium-sized and large bubbles were there altogether? ⬚ bubbles

Which bubble size were there most of? ....

Certificate

1st Grade

Congratulations to

....

for successfully finishing this book.

GOOD JOB!

You're a star.

☆ ☆ ☆ ☆ ☆

Date

....

Answer Section with Parents' Notes

This book is intended to teach math problem solving to first grade children. The content is designed to feature problems similar to those they may encounter in everyday life.

Contents

By working through this book, your child will practice:

- identifying numbers up to 120;
- using number lines to solve problems;
- solving addition problems using the commutative property;
- solving addition problems using the associative property and by making tens;
- identifying tens and ones;
- adding and subtracting two-digit numbers to solve problems;
- using standard and nonstandard measurements to solve problems;
- telling the time;
- using a calendar;
- identifying 2-D and 3-D shapes to solve problems;
- using and making picture graphs and bar graphs to solve problems.

How to Help Your Child

Guide your child by reading the problems and instructions slowly. Make sure he or she understands the questions, the concepts involved, and the different math terms being used.

As you work with your child, you will get an idea of what he or she finds easy, as well as what is more challenging. Use a hands-on approach to help your child understand any concepts he or she finds difficult to grasp. For example, use blocks or other objects found around the home to practice counting. It may also be useful to have a notebook or even a small chalkboard to jot down numbers and to draw on.

Remember to build your child's confidence by praising success. Encourage your child to persist when faced with small challenges. Always remember that finding solutions to math problems should be exciting.

GOAL: Learn the number words for 1 to 10.

Draw a line to match the number word on each balloon with the correct number from the list in the middle.

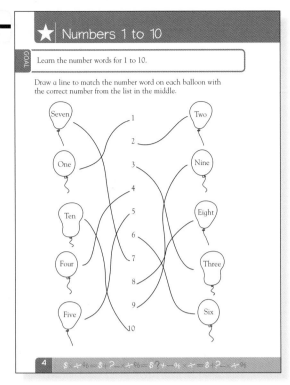

Seven, One, Ten, Four, Five — 1 2 3 4 5 6 7 8 9 10 — Two, Nine, Eight, Three, Six

4

Let your child practice saying numbers aloud in sequence. Reinforce this skill by counting numbers aloud with your child as you point to each number word.

GOAL: Learn the number words for 11 to 20.

Help Bruno the dog reach his doghouse. Find the bones that have the number words from 11 to 20 on them. Color them in to show Bruno the way.

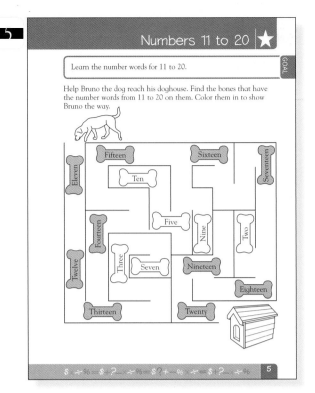

Fifteen, Sixteen, Seventeen, Eleven, Ten, Fourteen, Five, Nine, Two, Twelve, Three, Seven, Nineteen, Eighteen, Thirteen, Twenty

5

Help your child make the connection between number words and their symbols, or numerals. You can also let your child match number words or numerals to sets of items, such as ten marbles or 15 pencils.

★ Number Lines

GOAL: Learn to count along a number line.

Fill in the missing numbers on the number line below.

0 1 (2) (3) 4 (5) (6) 7 8 (9)

Now circle the correct number to answer these questions.

If you start at 3 and count forward two numbers, which number do you land on?
(5) 7 8

If you start at 0 and count forward three numbers, which number do you land on?
2 (3) 4

If you start at 5 and count forward four numbers, which number do you land on?
7 8 (9)

Find two even numbers on the line and write them here.
☐ ☐ Answers may vary

Find two odd numbers on the line and write them here.
☐ ☐ Answers may vary

6

Using a number line provides a visual foundation not only for counting but also for simple addition and subtraction problems.

Using Number Lines ★

GOAL: Learn to solve addition problems using a number line.

Jake, Sara, and Don visit the farmers' market with their dad. Count along the number line below to find the answer for each problem.

0 1 2 3 4 5 6 7 8 9

Dad buys two apples for Sara and three apples for Jake. How many apples is that altogether? [5] apples

For Halloween, Don would like a pumpkin for the front porch. Jake wants one for the back porch. Sara wants one for the front window. How many pumpkins should they ask their dad to buy? [3] pumpkins

Dad picks two big, juicy tomatoes from a stall and puts them in a bag. Sara adds two more tomatoes to the bag. How many tomatoes are in the bag altogether? [4] tomatoes

7

Draw a number line showing the numbers 0 to 9. Use items like paper bags, pencils, and cans of food to create problems of your own. Encourage your child to solve the problems using the number line.

★ Double-Digit Number Lines

Learn to use a number line with two-digit numbers.

Write the missing numbers on this number line.

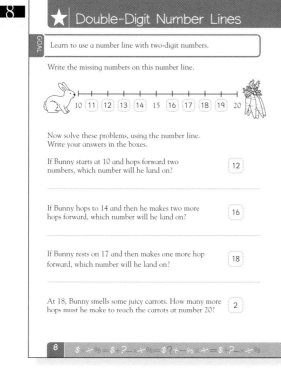

10 | 11 | 12 | 13 | 14 | 15 | 16 | 17 | 18 | 19 | 20

Now solve these problems, using the number line. Write your answers in the boxes.

If Bunny starts at 10 and hops forward two numbers, which number will he land on? **12**

If Bunny hops to 14 and then he makes two more hops forward, which number will he land on? **16**

If Bunny rests on 17 and then makes one more hop forward, which number will he land on? **18**

At 18, Bunny smells some juicy carrots. How many more hops must he make to reach the carrots at number 20? **2**

Using a number line helps your child compare greater and smaller numbers. Explain that numbers to the right are greater, while those to the left are smaller.

9

Double-Digit Number Lines ★

Practice counting two-digit numbers along a number line.

Use the number line to find the answers to the clues below.

10 11 12 13 14 15 16 17 18 19 20

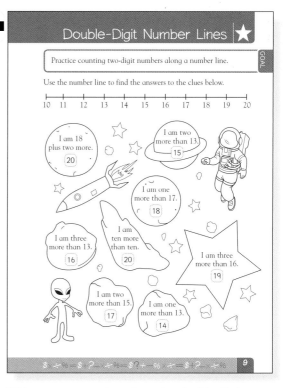

I am 18 plus two more. **20**

I am two more than 13. **15**

I am one more than 17. **18**

I am three more than 13. **16**

I am ten more than ten. **20**

I am three more than 16. **19**

I am two more than 15. **17**

I am one more than 13. **14**

Write some more clues that give double-digit numbers as answers. Then ask your child to use a number line to find the answers. Ask him or her to write answers from 10 to 19 in one color and answers from 20 onward in another color.

10

★ Using Number Lines

Learn to solve subtraction problems using a number line.

Chloe the cat has nine kittens. Help her keep track of them by filling in the missing number in each rhyme. Use the number line to figure out the answers.

0 1 2 3 4 5 6 7 8 9

Three kittens are playing, but one runs away.

Now just **2** of the kittens are left to play.

Five kittens are drinking from a pan.

But **3** take off to see a tall man.

Two of the kittens stay by the pan.

Seven kittens climb up a tree.

4 climb down.

And now the tree has three.

Nine kittens run outside chasing a mouse.

0 kittens are left in the house.

Explain to your child that when subtracting, he or she must count left from the greater number. This demonstrates how subtraction is the "taking away" of a number or quantity of objects.

11

Using Number Lines ★

Practice subtraction with a double-digit number line.

The Rams basketball team has won six games in a row. The scores are given below. Count backward on the number line to figure out the difference in points scored in each game.

10 11 12 13 14 15 16 17 18 19 20

Game 1
Rams **17** Visitors **6**
Difference **11**

Game 2
Rams **15** Visitors **5**
Difference **10**

Game 3
Rams **20** Visitors **7**
Difference **13**

Game 4
Rams **15** Visitors **1**
Difference **14**

Game 5
Rams **18** Visitors **2**
Difference **16**

Game 6
Rams **20** Visitors **10**
Difference **10**

Now answer these questions.

Which game shows a difference of 14 points? **Game 4**

Which game has a difference of 11 points? **Game 1**

Which game did the Rams win by the most points? **Game 5**

Explain to your child that to subtract, he or she should move back along the line the number of places that are to be subtracted. The number he or she lands on is the answer.

★ Add Three Numbers

GOAL Learn to solve problems that involve adding three numbers.

Flash the fish is swimming through the salty sea.

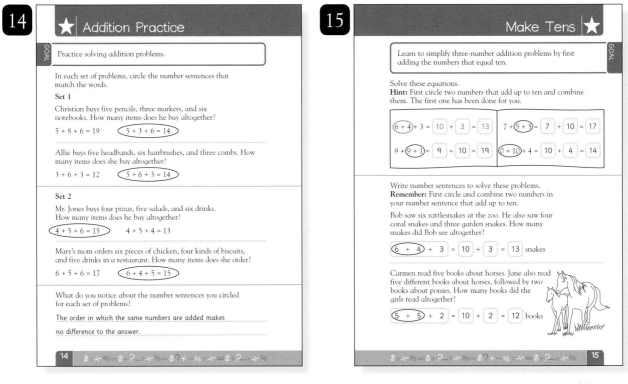

Write out the number sentence to solve each of these problems.

Four whales swim up to Flash. Then four rays arrive, followed by two clown fish. How many sea animals are with Flash now?

$4 + 4 + 2 = 10$ sea animals

Flash swims past three sea anemones. He then sees five more sea anemones. Later, he spots another four. How many sea anemones does Flash see in all?

$3 + 5 + 4 = 12$ sea anemones

Flash sees 15 starfish on the ocean floor. Then he spots two jellyfish and a small blue fish next to them. How many sea animals does Flash see on the ocean floor?

$15 + 2 + 1 = 18$ sea animals

When adding three numbers, your child may find one of these strategies helpful: adding the greater numbers first; adding up any doubles first; or adding up numbers that make a total of ten first.

Number Order ★

GOAL Learn about number order when adding.

Write the answers to each pair of equations. **Note:** The numbers being added are the same in each pair.

$7 + 2 + 1 = 10$ $2 + 7 + 1 = 10$

$6 + 1 + 0 = 7$ $0 + 6 + 1 = 7$

$5 + 3 + 1 = 9$ $3 + 1 + 5 = 9$

What do the answers tell you about the order of numbers (or addends) in an addition problem?

The order you add numbers in makes no difference to the answer.

Carrie and Mack go to a carnival.

Carrie takes two rides on the Ferris wheel, one ride on the Space Blaster, and three rides on the Tilt-a-Whirl.

Mack takes three rides on the Ferris wheel. Then he rides the Tilt-a-Whirl twice and the Space Blaster once. Who takes the most rides? **Hint:** First write the number sentences to arrive at the answer.

Carrie's rides   Mack's rides

$2 + 1 + 3 = 6$ $3 + 2 + 1 = 6$

Both take the same number of rides.

Provide your child with additional problems involving the addition of three numbers. Change the order of the numbers being added for each equation. Explain to your child that the order of numbers in an addition equation does not affect the result. This is called the "commutative property."

★ Addition Practice

GOAL Practice solving addition problems.

In each set of problems, circle the number sentences that match the words.

Set 1

Christian buys five pencils, three markers, and six notebooks. How many items does he buy altogether?

$5 + 8 + 6 = 19$ $(5 + 3 + 6 = 14)$

Allie buys five headbands, six hairbrushes, and three combs. How many items does she buy altogether?

$3 + 6 + 3 = 12$ $(5 + 6 + 3 = 14)$

Set 2

Mr. Jones buys four pizzas, five salads, and six drinks. How many items does he buy altogether?

$(4 + 5 + 6 = 15)$ $4 + 5 + 4 = 13$

Mary's mom orders six pieces of chicken, four kinds of biscuits, and five drinks in a restaurant. How many items does she order?

$6 + 5 + 6 = 17$ $(6 + 4 + 5 = 15)$

What do you notice about the number sentences you circled for each set of problems?

The order in which the same numbers are added makes

no difference to the answer.

This page reinforces the work done on page 13, making sure your child understands that the order in which numbers are added makes no difference to the total.

Make Tens ★

GOAL Learn to simplify three-number addition problems by first adding the numbers that equal ten.

Solve these equations.
Hint: First circle two numbers that add up to ten and combine them. The first one has been done for you.

$(6 + 4) + 3 = 10 + 3 = 13$ $7 + (5 + 5) = 7 + 10 = 17$

$9 + (9 + 1) = 9 + 10 = 19$ $(0 + 10) + 4 = 10 + 4 = 14$

Write number sentences to solve these problems.
Remember: First circle and combine two numbers in your number sentence that add up to ten.

Bob saw six rattlesnakes at the zoo. He also saw four coral snakes and three garden snakes. How many snakes did Bob see altogether?

$(6 + 4) + 3 = 10 + 3 = 13$ snakes

Carmen read five books about horses. Jane also read five different books about horses, followed by two books about ponies. How many books did the girls read altogether?

$(5 + 5) + 2 = 10 + 2 = 12$ books

Place ten objects, such as marbles, on a table. Have your child close his or her eyes. Remove some objects. Ask him or her to count the remaining objects and say how many you removed. This game teaches your child the different ways two numbers can make ten.

★ Count by Tens

GOAL | Learn to count by tens.

Four crows are gathering twigs to build their nests. Solve these problems. Show your work in the box. The first one has been done for you.

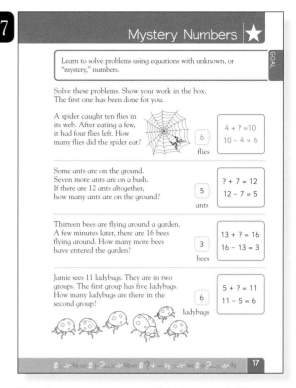

Each crow gathers a bundle of ten twigs. How many twigs do they collect altogether?

40 twigs

> 4 bundles of 10 =
> 10 + 10 + 10 + 10
> = 40

One crow uses her bundle of twigs to build a nest. How many unused twigs do the crows now have altogether?

30 twigs

> 1 bundle =
> 10 twigs
> 40 – 10 = 30

Another crow decides to make a larger nest. She uses twice as many twigs as the first crow did. How many twigs does she use?

20 twigs

> 2 bundles of 10 =
> 10 + 10 = 20

The four crows go out to gather more twigs. This time they collect two bundles of ten sticks each. How many twigs is that altogether?

80 twigs

> 8 bundles of 10 =
> 10 + 10 + 10 + 10 +
> 10 + 10 + 10 + 10
> = 80

To reinforce familiarity with groups of tens, say aloud a number such as 30, which is a multiple of ten. Ask your child how many tens there are in the number. If necessary, draw objects in groups of tens to show how many make up the number.

Mystery Numbers ★

GOAL | Learn to solve problems using equations with unknown, or "mystery," numbers.

Solve these problems. Show your work in the box. The first one has been done for you.

A spider caught ten flies in its web. After eating a few, it had four flies left. How many flies did the spider eat?

6 flies

> 4 + ? = 10
> 10 – 4 = 6

Some ants are on the ground. Seven more ants are on a bush. If there are 12 ants altogether, how many ants are on the ground?

5 ants

> ? + 7 = 12
> 12 – 7 = 5

Thirteen bees are flying around a garden. A few minutes later, there are 16 bees flying around. How many more bees have entered the garden?

3 bees

> 13 + ? = 16
> 16 – 13 = 3

Jamie sees 11 ladybugs. They are in two groups. The first group has five ladybugs. How many ladybugs are there in the second group?

6 ladybugs

> 5 + ? = 11
> 11 – 5 = 6

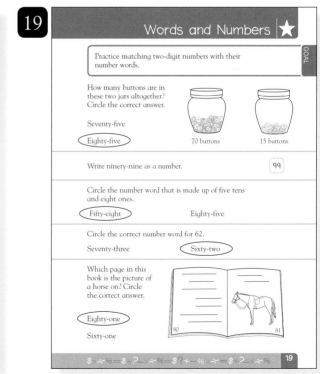

Visualizing an equation will help your child find a missing number in it. Let him or her draw or use sets of objects to represent the equation. Understanding sets of things and their relationships is fundamental to solving math problems.

★ Numbers Up to 120

GOAL | Learn to count and write numbers up to 120.

Karl has a bucket of berries for his pet parrot. Help him reach his pet by filling in the missing numbers on the stones along his path.

Draw a grid and write the number 25 in the box in the top left corner. Have your child fill in the progression of numbers up to 120. Then start at 120 and ask him or her to count back to 25. It will help reinforce number order.

Words and Numbers ★

GOAL | Practice matching two-digit numbers with their number words.

How many buttons are in these two jars altogether? Circle the correct answer.

Seventy-five

(Eighty-five)

70 buttons   15 buttons

Write ninety-nine as a number.

99

Circle the number word that is made up of five tens and eight ones.

(Fifty-eight)   Eighty-five

Circle the correct number word for 62.

Seventy-three   (Sixty-two)

Which page in this book is the picture of a horse on? Circle the correct answer.

(Eighty-one)

Sixty-one

80   81

Understanding the place values of tens and ones helps your child understand which values are greater than and less than one another. This will help with problem solving, especially when your child moves on to working with place values of hundreds and thousands.

★ More or Less

GOAL Learn to use the symbols for greater than (>) and less than (<) to compare numbers.

Look at the numbers on each pair of fish below. Then write the correct symbol to compare the numbers.

15 < 33   61 > 60

45 > 38   38 > 32

19 < 56   42 < 50

27 > 14   25 > 15

63 < 99   72 < 82

Look at the fish again. If a fish has a number that is greater than 30, color it in.

The aim of the activity on this page is to help your child understand that two-digit numbers consist of groups of tens and ones.

Two-Digit Numbers ★

GOAL Learn three ways to represent two-digit numbers.

Fill in the empty boxes on the chart.

Word	Numeral	Blocks
Thirty-two	32	
Twenty-five	25	
Sixteen	16	
Sixty-three	63	

Get your child to explain how he or she would teach the meaning of tens and ones to another child of the same age. This will reinforce the concept of tens and ones. Offer guidance if necessary.

★ Tens and Ones

GOAL Learn about the place values of tens and ones in two-digit numbers. For example, the numeral 23 is made up of 2 tens and 3 ones.

Tens | Ones
2 | 3 = 23

These children are learning about place values. On the table are small blocks to represent ones and longer blocks to represent tens.

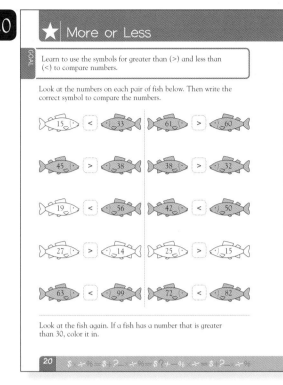

Todd uses the blocks on the table to make a model for the number 27. He lays out two long blocks to show 2 tens. How many small blocks must he add to show the ones?

7 small blocks

The teacher shows the children a drawing of some dots to illustrate the number 87. Her drawing shows seven dots for the ones. How many rows of ten dots does it show?

8 rows

Charlene writes the number 45 on a piece of paper. She then draws some dots to illustrate the number. She draws a group of five dots for the ones. What else must she draw to illustrate the number 45?

Charlene must also draw four rows of ten dots.

Do the numbers 14 and 41 have the same number of tens and ones?

No. 14 has 1 ten and 4 ones, but 41 has 4 tens and 1 one.

This exercise of splitting each number to be added into tens and ones will help your child understand how addition works. Many children find this concept difficult to understand; remind your child to be patient and work through each problem carefully.

Tens and Ones ★

GOAL Learn about place value in two-digit numbers.

These pirates are digging for treasure. Treasure boxes, buried deep in the sand, contain gold. Each box has a code on it showing how much treasure is inside it. Use the key to work out how many bars of gold are in each box.

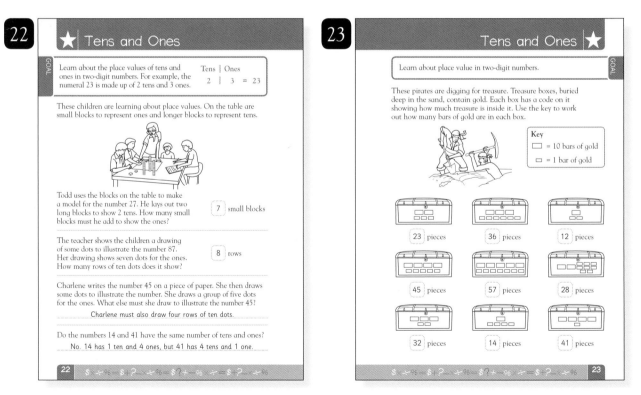

Key
▭ = 10 bars of gold
▫ = 1 bar of gold

23 pieces   36 pieces   12 pieces

45 pieces   57 pieces   28 pieces

32 pieces   14 pieces   41 pieces

Again splitting numbers into tens and ones will help your child to be more confident and accurate when subtracting two-digit numbers. Remind your child to always check his or her answers.

★ Ten More or Ten Less

GOAL: Learn to identify ten more or ten less than a two-digit number.

Draw a line to match each spaceship to the star with the correct answer.

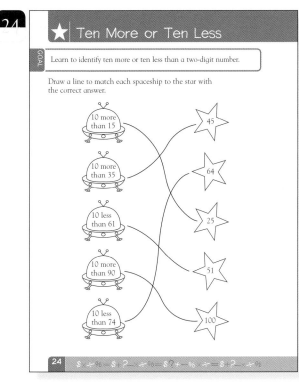

10 more than 15 → 25
10 more than 35 → 45
10 less than 61 → 51
10 more than 90 → 100
10 less than 74 → 64

Stars: 45, 64, 25, 51, 100

Being able to calculate ten more or ten less than a number helps your child solve addition and subtraction problems quickly. This will also be useful when solving more difficult number operations, such as multiplication and division.

Ten More or Ten Less ★

GOAL: Practice solving problems by calculating ten more or ten less than a two-digit number.

Solve these problems. Try to use mental math to figure out the answers, if you can.

Juan counts 22 birds in the branches of a tree. He then sees another ten birds flying by. How many birds does Juan see altogether?　**32** birds

Jane counts 18 fence posts as she rides her bicycle down the street. As she rides back, she counts ten more fence posts on the other side of the street. How many fence posts does Jane count altogether?　**28** fence posts

Mike counts 13 yellow flowers in his garden and ten yellow flowers in his neighbor's garden. How many yellow flowers does he count altogether?　**23** yellow flowers

Shep spots 16 butterflies near a path. Ten of them fly away. How many butterflies are left?　**6** butterflies

Jason sees 12 squirrels near a tree. As Jason approaches, ten of them run away. How many squirrels are left?　**2** squirrels

Spend some extra time saying numbers aloud to your child and having him or her calculate mentally ten more or ten less than each number. Ask your child to say the answers aloud. Saying, instead of writing, will help reinforce his or her mental agility for real-life problem solving.

★ Add Two-Digit Numbers

GOAL: Practice addition with two-digit numbers.
Hint: First add the ones together, then add the tens.

$$\begin{array}{r} 2|2 \\ +1|4 \\ \hline 6 \end{array} \rightarrow \begin{array}{r} 2|2 \\ +1|4 \\ \hline 3\ 6 \end{array}$$

Write the answers.

$$\begin{array}{r} 42 \\ +20 \\ \hline 62 \end{array} \qquad \begin{array}{r} 31 \\ +51 \\ \hline 82 \end{array} \qquad \begin{array}{r} 45 \\ +32 \\ \hline 77 \end{array} \qquad \begin{array}{r} 12 \\ +33 \\ \hline 45 \end{array} \qquad \begin{array}{r} 10 \\ +15 \\ \hline 25 \end{array}$$

Now solve these problems. Show your work in the box.

Pete stacks 70 cans of peas on the shelves of his store. He also stacks 24 cans of corn. How many cans does Pete stack altogether?

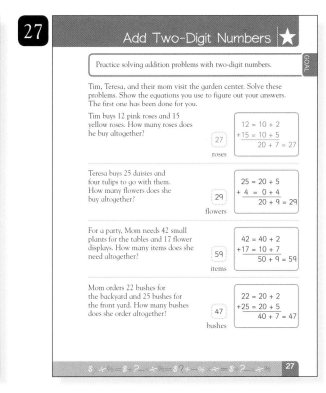

$$\begin{array}{r} 70 \\ +24 \\ \hline 94 \end{array}$$

94 cans

Pete moves and restacks 50 cans of tomatoes to make room for another 30 cans, which he adds to the shelf. How many cans does he move and stack in all?

$$\begin{array}{r} 50 \\ +30 \\ \hline 80 \end{array}$$

80 cans

Place value is the value of a digit depending on its position in a number. Understanding the place-value system very well is essential to your child's progress in solving math problems.

Add Two-Digit Numbers ★

GOAL: Practice solving addition problems with two-digit numbers.

Tim, Teresa, and their mom visit the garden center. Solve these problems. Show the equations you use to figure out your answers. The first one has been done for you.

Tim buys 12 pink roses and 15 yellow roses. How many roses does he buy altogether?　**27** roses

$$\begin{array}{r} 12 = 10 + 2 \\ +15 = 10 + 5 \\ \hline 20 + 7 = 27 \end{array}$$

Teresa buys 25 daisies and four tulips to go with them. How many flowers does she buy altogether?　**29** flowers

$$\begin{array}{r} 25 = 20 + 5 \\ +\ 4 = 0 + 4 \\ \hline 20 + 9 = 29 \end{array}$$

For a party, Mom needs 42 small plants for the tables and 17 flower displays. How many items does she need altogether?　**59** items

$$\begin{array}{r} 42 = 40 + 2 \\ +17 = 10 + 7 \\ \hline 50 + 9 = 59 \end{array}$$

Mom orders 22 bushes for the backyard and 25 bushes for the front yard. How many bushes does she order altogether?　**47** bushes

$$\begin{array}{r} 22 = 20 + 2 \\ +25 = 20 + 5 \\ \hline 40 + 7 = 47 \end{array}$$

Your child must be able to read and understand numerals and number words quickly to solve math problems. He or she must be familiar with the pattern of ones and tens and be able to read them correctly as two-digit numbers.

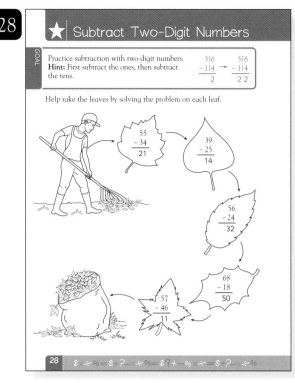

★ Subtract Two-Digit Numbers

GOAL

Practice subtraction with two-digit numbers.
Hint: First subtract the ones, then subtract the tens.

$$\begin{array}{r} 3|6 \\ -1|4 \\ \hline 2 \end{array} \rightarrow \begin{array}{r} 3|6 \\ -1|4 \\ \hline 2\,2 \end{array}$$

Help rake the leaves by solving the problem on each leaf.

$$\begin{array}{r} 55 \\ -34 \\ \hline 21 \end{array}$$

$$\begin{array}{r} 39 \\ -25 \\ \hline 14 \end{array}$$

$$\begin{array}{r} 56 \\ -24 \\ \hline 32 \end{array}$$

$$\begin{array}{r} 68 \\ -18 \\ \hline 50 \end{array}$$

$$\begin{array}{r} 57 \\ -46 \\ \hline 11 \end{array}$$

As your child solves two-digit addition problems, remind him or her to first add the ones, then the tens. Learning this process will enable your child to solve problems more readily when he or she later works with three-digit problems.

Subtract Two-Digit Numbers ★

GOAL

Practice solving subtraction problems with two-digit numbers.

Some friends collect baseball game tickets, baseball cards, and baseballs. Solve these problems. Show your work in the box. The first one has been done for you.

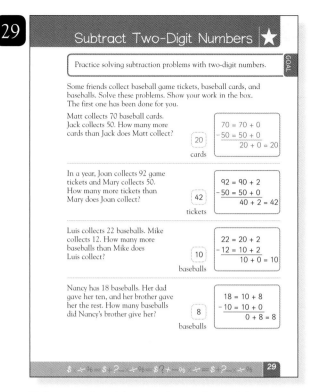

Matt collects 70 baseball cards. Jack collects 50. How many more cards than Jack does Matt collect?

20 cards

$$\begin{array}{r} 70 = 70 + 0 \\ -50 = 50 + 0 \\ \hline 20 + 0 = 20 \end{array}$$

In a year, Joan collects 92 game tickets and Mary collects 50. How many more tickets than Mary does Joan collect?

42 tickets

$$\begin{array}{r} 92 = 90 + 2 \\ -50 = 50 + 0 \\ \hline 40 + 2 = 42 \end{array}$$

Luis collects 22 baseballs. Mike collects 12. How many more baseballs than Mike does Luis collect?

10 baseballs

$$\begin{array}{r} 22 = 20 + 2 \\ -12 = 10 + 2 \\ \hline 10 + 0 = 10 \end{array}$$

Nancy has 18 baseballs. Her dad gave her ten, and her brother gave her the rest. How many baseballs did Nancy's brother give her?

8 baseballs

$$\begin{array}{r} 18 = 10 + 8 \\ -10 = 10 + 0 \\ \hline 0 + 8 = 8 \end{array}$$

Before starting this page, it may be useful to review subtraction involving single-digit numbers. This basic understanding of subtraction will give your child the skills needed to subtract two-digit numbers quickly and accurately.

★ Money

GOAL

Learn the names and values of coins.

1¢ Penny 5¢ Nickel 10¢ Dime 25¢ Quarter 50¢ Half-dollar

For each row, circle the coin on the right that has the same value as the total number of coins on the left.

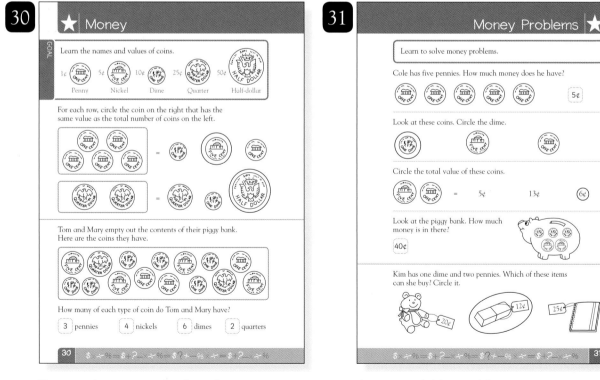

Tom and Mary empty out the contents of their piggy bank. Here are the coins they have.

How many of each type of coin do Tom and Mary have?

3 pennies   4 nickels   6 dimes   2 quarters

Knowing the names and values of coins is an important skill, and one that your child may not yet have learned. Be patient with your child while reviewing the names of the coins and the values they represent.

Money Problems ★

GOAL

Learn to solve money problems.

Cole has five pennies. How much money does he have?

5¢

Look at these coins. Circle the dime.

Circle the total value of these coins.

= 5¢   13¢   (6¢)

Look at the piggy bank. How much money is in there?

40¢

Kim has one dime and two pennies. Which of these items can she buy? Circle it.

20¢   12¢   25¢

Once your child is confident in recognizing coins and their value, show him or her a dollar bill. Explain that it has a value of 100 ¢ and show him or her the coins that add up to the same value as a dollar bill.

★ Measure Length

Learn to measure length using a common object, such as a penny.

Baseball bats are lying on the floor.

Bat 1

Bat 2

Bat 3

Use a penny to measure each bat and answer these questions.

Which bat is the longest? How long is it?

Bat 3 — 7 pennies long

Which bat is the shortest? How long is it?

Bat 1 — 5 pennies long

Which bat is 6 pennies long?

Bat 2

Using pennies as nonstandard measuring tools is a good way to introduce your child to the concept of length. It will help him or her think mathematically about the things in everyday life. Other nonstandard tools could include toothpicks, index cards, and paper clips.

Measure in Inches ★

Learn to measure length in inches.

Use a ruler marked in inches to find the length of these objects.

4 inches

2 inches

5 inches

3 inches

Now answer these questions.

Which object is the longest? — Marker

Which object is the shortest? — Eraser

Which object is 4 inches long? — Pencil

Help your child use a ruler marked in inches to measure items around the home, such as the height of a drinking glass or the length of a spoon. Explain the difference between length and height. Make sure your child uses the correct terms when measuring—for example, "2 inches high" and "4 inches long."

★ Measure in Centimeters

Learn to measure length in centimeters.

Ruby loves ribbons. Use a ruler marked in centimeters to help her measure these ribbons for her hair.

7 centimeters

10 centimeters

12 centimeters

Look at these ribbons and then answer the questions.

3 cm

7 cm

10 cm

How many of the ribbons shown above are longer than 6 centimeters? — 2 ribbons

How many of the ribbons shown above are shorter than 8 centimeters? — 2 ribbons

Ruby needs a piece of ribbon that is 10 centimeters long. Which of the ribbons shown above can she use? Circle it.

Using a centimeter ruler will introduce your child to the metric system of measurement. Together, practice measuring household objects with the ruler and compare the results when you measure the same objects in inches.

Measuring Tools ★

Learn about different measurement tools and their uses.

Weight	Volume	Temperature	Length
Scale	Measuring cup	Thermometer	Ruler

Circle the correct picture to answer each question.

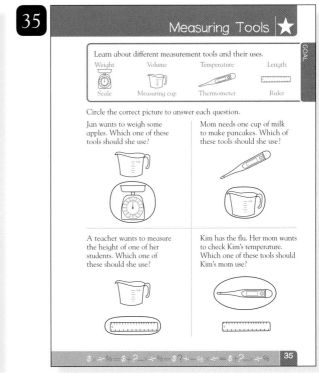

Jan wants to weigh some apples. Which one of these tools should she use?

Mom needs one cup of milk to make pancakes. Which of these tools should she use?

A teacher wants to measure the height of one of her students. Which one of these should she use?

Kim has the flu. Her mom wants to check Kim's temperature. Which one of these tools should Kim's mom use?

Your child's knowledge of measurement tools allows him or her to understand and compare physical attributes of things. This knowledge, along with the correct measurement tools, gives your child a variety of ways to solve problems.

★ Time

GOAL

Learn to tell the time to the hour and the half hour.

2:00	3:30
Two o'clock	Three thirty

Show the correct time to match the statements given below. First draw the hands on the analog clock. Then write the time on the digital clock.

Grumpy the groundhog gets up at 7 o'clock. | 7:00

Ronnie the rabbit has his breakfast at 8 o'clock. | 8:00

Suzy the squirrel wakes up at five thirty. | 5:30

Pearl the peacock takes her nap at one thirty. | 1:30

Discuss with your child how we measure time in minutes and hours. Relating a period of time to how long he or she takes to perform an activity, such as eating breakfast, brushing teeth, or playing, will help your child understand time better.

Time ★

GOAL

Practice telling the time. **Note:** When you say "half past one," it is the same as saying "one thirty."

Match the times written in the box below to the correct clock image. Write the correct time underneath each clock.

11:30	Seven thirty	8:30	2 o'clock	4:00
Nine thirty	10 o'clock	Two thirty	Twelve thirty

Nine thirty | Two thirty | Twelve thirty

2 o'clock | Seven thirty | 10 o'clock

11:30 | 8:30 | 4:00

Learning to tell the time and knowing the different ways in which it is expressed will help your child understand math concepts, such as fractions, better.

★ Using a Calendar

GOAL

Learn to read a calendar.

Look at the calendar page below. Then answer the questions that follow.

July

Sunday	Monday	Tuesday	Wednesday	Thursday	Friday	Saturday
		1	2	3	Independence Day 4	5
6	7	8	9	10	11	12
13	14	15	16	17	18	19
20	21	22	23	24	25	26
27	28	29	30	31		

How many Sundays are in the month shown? | 4

Tom's birthday is on July 12. Jo's birthday is on July 16. How many days later than Tom's birthday is Jo's? | 4 days

Which day of the week is July 1? | Tuesday

Which day comes between Wednesday and Friday? | Thursday

It is July 22. In three days, Mrs. Lee's class is going on a picnic. What day is the picnic on? What will the date be? | Friday, 25 July

Using a calendar with your child helps reinforce reading, sequencing, and counting skills, while familiarizing him or her with the days of the week and the months of the year.

Using a Calendar ★

GOAL

Practice using a calendar.

Use this calendar page to answer the questions below.

September

Sunday	Monday	Tuesday	Wednesday	Thursday	Friday	Saturday
				1	2	3
4	5	6	7	8	9	10
11	12	13	14	15	16	17
18	19	20	21	22	23	24
25	26	27	28	29	30	

How many days are in September? | 30 days

How many Fridays are in this month? | 5

September 8 is Mary's fourth day back at school after summer vacation. On which day and date did school start? | Monday, September 5

Mark has soccer practice in two days. Today is September 6. On what day and date does Mark have soccer practice? | Thursday, September 8

This page reinforces the skills acquired by working through the activities on page 38. Build on your child's skills by giving him or her a calendar of the current month and asking questions of your own.

GOAL

Learn to identify some common 2-D shapes.

| Square | Triangle | Oval | Circle | Rectangle |

Fill in the missing word in each speech bubble.

I see a shape with four corners and four straight sides. The sides are not all the same length, but opposite sides are. It is a __rectangle__.

I see a shape with four corners and four sides that are the same length. It is a __square__.

I see a shape that looks like an egg. It has no corners. It is an __oval__.

I see a shape that has three sides and three corners. It is a __triangle__.

I see a round shape. It has no corners. It is a __circle__.

40

Explain to your child the properties of shapes, such as the number of sides and corners they have and whether the sides are straight lines or curves.

GOAL

Learn to identify 2-D shapes in the world around you.

Look at these pictures on the wall of an art gallery. They are displayed in a variety of frames. How many frames of each shape can you see? Add this information to the chart below.

Shape	□	△	⬭	○	▭
Number	2	4	2	6	2

Now answer these questions.

Which shape is there the most of? _____ Circle

Which three shapes have two frames each? _____ Square, Oval, and Rectangle

Four of the frames are this shape. Which shape is it? _____ Triangle

41

Help your child compare shapes by asking questions such as "How are they alike?" and "How are they different?" Talk about size, showing that the same shape can come in many different sizes. This will help your child develop a strong foundation for the study of geometry in later grades.

42

GOAL

Learn to identify some common 3-D shapes.

| Cone | Sphere | Cube | Pyramid | Cylinder | Rectangular prism |

Some of the 3-D shapes in this maze have the wrong labels. Find your way through the maze by following only the 3-D shapes with the correct labels.

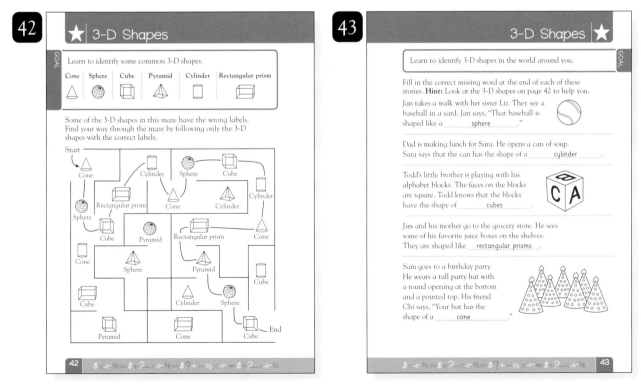

Start

Cone, Cylinder, Sphere, Cube, Cylinder, Sphere, Rectangular prism, Cone, Cylinder, Cube, Pyramid, Rectangular prism, Cone, Cone, Sphere, Pyramid, Cube, Cube, Cylinder, Sphere, Pyramid, Cone, Cube, End

42

Explain to your child that some 3-D shapes have faces (flat areas), sides (edges), and corners, while others do not. Let your child compare different 3-D shapes, and ask him or her to figure out how many faces, sides, and corners each one has.

43

GOAL

Learn to identify 3-D shapes in the world around you.

Fill in the correct missing word at the end of each of these stories. **Hint:** Look at the 3-D shapes on page 42 to help you.

Jan takes a walk with her sister Liz. They see a baseball in a yard. Jan says, "That baseball is shaped like a __sphere__."

Dad is making lunch for Sara. He opens a can of soup. Sara says that the can has the shape of a __cylinder__.

Todd's little brother is playing with his alphabet blocks. The faces on the blocks are square. Todd knows that the blocks have the shape of __cubes__.

Jim and his mother go to the grocery store. He sees some of his favorite juice boxes on the shelves. They are shaped like __rectangular prisms__.

Sam goes to a birthday party. He wears a tall party hat with a round opening at the bottom and a pointed top. His friend Chi says, "Your hat has the shape of a __cone__."

43

Take a walk around your neighborhood with your child. Ask him or her to point out objects that match the 3-D shapes he or she has learned. Connecting shapes with the real objects will help your child with concepts used in geometry.

★ Picture Graphs

GOAL Learn to use a picture graph to find information.

A class of first grade children were offered fruit after lunch. They had a choice of a banana, an apple, a pear, or an orange. The picture graph below shows how many children ate each type of fruit.

Fruit Children Ate   ☺ = 1 child

Type of Fruit	Number of Children
Banana	☺ ☺ ☺ ☺ ☺
Apple	☺ ☺ ☺ ☺
Pear	☺ ☺ ☺
Orange	☺ ☺ ☺

Use the information on the picture graph to answer these questions.

Which type of fruit did most of the children choose? **Banana**

How many children ate a banana? **5** children

How many children ate an apple? **4** children

How many more children had a banana than had an orange? **2** children

How many children altogether ate fruit after their lunch? **15** children

Look through magazines, newspapers, or the Internet with your child for examples of picture graphs. Ask him or her if he or she can explain to you the information that they show.

Picture Graphs ★

GOAL Learn how to show information on a picture graph.

In a school survey, a class of first graders voted for their favorite pizza. Four children voted for cheese pizza. One child chose mushroom pizza. Three chose pepperoni pizza and two chose sausage pizza. Complete the picture graph below to show how many children voted for each type of pizza. Give your graph a title.

Favorite Types of Pizza   ☺ = 1 child

Type of Pizza	Number of Children
Cheese	☺ ☺ ☺ ☺
Mushroom	☺
Pepperoni	☺ ☺ ☺
Sausage	☺ ☺

Use your picture graph to help you answer these questions.

Which type of pizza was the least popular? **Mushroom**

Which type of pizza did most children choose? **Cheese**

How many types of pizza does the graph show? **4**

How many more children chose cheese pizza than chose mushroom pizza? **3** children

Graphs visually display information about objects or situations. On a picture graph, your child sees that pictures stand for real objects, so that the information can be easily interpreted.

★ Bar Graphs

GOAL Learn to find information by looking at a bar graph.

A teacher asked her students to tell her their favorite toy. She then made a bar graph to show the results.

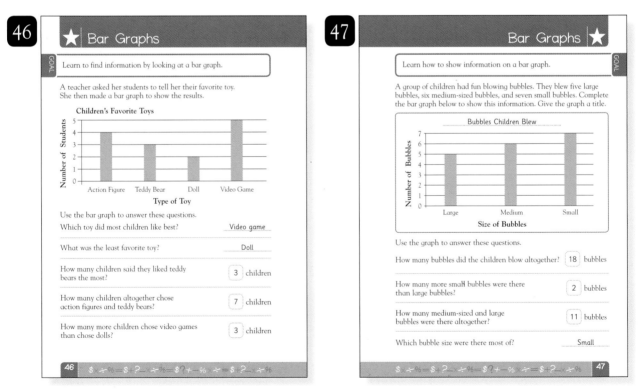

Children's Favorite Toys

Use the bar graph to answer these questions.

Which toy did most children like best? **Video game**

What was the least favorite toy? **Doll**

How many children said they liked teddy bears the most? **3** children

How many children altogether chose action figures and teddy bears? **7** children

How many more children chose video games than chose dolls? **3** children

Another word for the information presented on a graph is "data." Encourage your child to use this term. It will help him or her develop further competency in creating graphs in later grades.

Bar Graphs ★

GOAL Learn how to show information on a bar graph.

A group of children had fun blowing bubbles. They blew five large bubbles, six medium-sized bubbles, and seven small bubbles. Complete the bar graph below to show this information. Give the graph a title.

Bubbles Children Blew

Use the graph to answer these questions.

How many bubbles did the children blow altogether? **18** bubbles

How many more small bubbles were there than large bubbles? **2** bubbles

How many medium-sized and large bubbles were there altogether? **11** bubbles

Which bubble size were there most of? **Small**

Bar graphs are a great way to compare and understand data. Ensure your child is aware of the importance of the title of the graph and the labels on each axis, and uses that information to aid his or her understanding.